Money in the Bank

by Noah Jackson

Editorial Offices: Glenview, Illinois • Parsippany, New Jersey • New York, New York
Sales Offices: Needham, Massachusetts • Duluth, Georgia • Glenview, Illinois
Coppell, Texas • Sacramento, California • Mesa, Arizona

Penny		$0.01
Nickel		$0.05
Dime		$0.10
Quarter		$0.25
Dollar		$1.00

Do you have money at home? Maybe you have some dollar bills, some quarters, dimes, nickels, and pennies. If you do, you might want to put that money in a bank. A bank is a place that keeps money safe.

teller

When you go to the bank, you will see workers called *tellers.* A teller will take your money and help you start a *savings account.* The money in your savings account belongs only to you. No one else can take money out of your account— unless you tell them to!

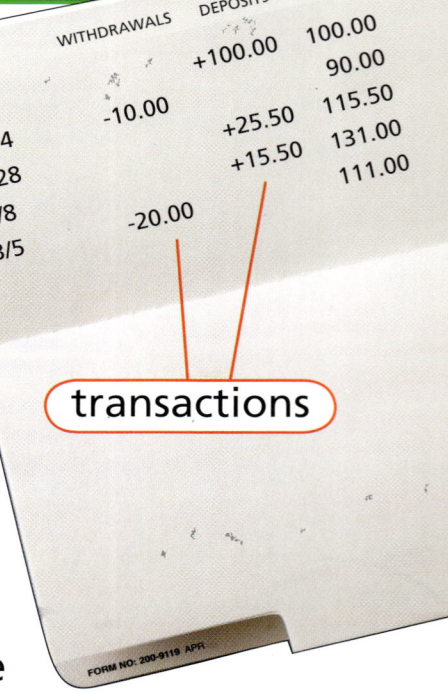

DATE	WITHDRAWALS	DEPOSITS	BALANCE	TELLER
		+100.00	100.00	
			90.00	
1/2	-10.00		115.50	
1/14		+25.50	131.00	
1/28		+15.50	111.00	
2/8				
3/5	-20.00			

FORM NO: 200-9119 APR

passbook

transactions

In some banks, the teller will give you a *passbook* when you start a savings account. This special book shows how much money you have in your savings account. The money in your account is called the *balance.*

4

You can put money into your savings account or take money out. When you put money into your savings account, it is called a *deposit*. When you take money out, it is called a *withdrawal.*

Deposits and withdrawals are called *transactions.* The balance changes each time you do a transaction.

statement

Banks help you keep track of how much money you have in your account. Each month your bank sends you a *statement*. A statement is a report that shows every transaction you did during the past month.

Some banks mail statements. Some send them by e-mail. Others let you look at your statements <mark>online</mark>, using a computer.

Did you know that banks may pay you money? This money is called *interest.* The bank pays you interest when you keep your money in the savings account for a long time.

---

online: available on computer, such as on the Internet

7

A bank can be helpful when you want to save money. Your money is safe. You can add money to your savings account. You can take money out of your account. And the bank may pay you money.

So it is smart to save money at a bank!